Up the River:

An Anthology

Up the River:
An Anthology

Poetry by Chandra Bozelko

Edited by Susan Nagelsen & Charles Huckelbury

Cover Art by Rachel Ternes
Cover Design by Liz Calka

Text Design by Sonia Tabriz

BleakHouse Publishing
2013

BleakHouse Publishing
Ward Circle Building 254
American University
Washington, D.C. 20016

NEC Box 67
New England College
Henniker, New Hampshire 03242
www.BleakHousePublishing.com

Robert Johnson – Editor & Publisher
Sonia Tabriz – Managing Editor
Liz Calka – Art Director

Rachel Cupelo – Marketing Director
Shirin Karimi – Senior Creative Consultant
Carla Mavaddat – Curator

Joanna Heaney – Chief Operating Officer
Alexa Kelly – Chief Editorial Officer
Nora Kirk – Chief Development Officer

ISBN-13: 978-0-9837769-6-3

Printed in the United States of America

Table of Contents

Acknowledgments

About the Author
About the Editors
About the Designers

Acknowledgements

No one ever goes up the river alone. I owe many thanks to my editor, Susan Nagelsen, who turned my amateur attempts at poetry into something that can convey the reality of prison to people who have never been here. Susan has a unique understanding of the vagaries of prison life, and it has bestowed a patience on her that few others have. I have been fortunate to be a beneficiary of Susan's expertise and kindness. Without her, I would be up the river with this book.

Robert Johnson, professor at American University and founder of BleakHouse Publishing, has helped not only me with the publication of this book but all incarcerated persons by giving us a voice. Many publishing houses and publications refuse even to entertain submissions from prisoners, but BleakHouse has dedicated itself to providing prisoners a platform, a very courageous stand to take. On behalf of all prisoners, I thank Professor Johnson and all the editors at BleakHouse who donate their time for acknowledging that society's underbelly has something worthwhile to say.

I would like to thank Mary O'Connor, poet and author of *Dreams of a Wingless Child*, who taught a poetry class here at York Correctional Institution. Mary introduced me to different styles and aesthetics of writing and in the process nudged me into thinking I might write something worth reading. Thank you, Mary, for that boost in my confidence.

Mary would never have graced this prison compound were it not for the continued sainthood of Joseph M. Lea, the prison's librarian. Mr. Lea works tirelessly to bring educational and enrichment opportunities to the residents of York under a prison administration that very often discourages intellectual growth.

Wally Lamb, my writing teacher for the past three years in the York Writing Group, has honed my writing and thinking so dramatically that I wonder how readers muddled through my pre-Wally writing. Thank you, Wally, for the guidance and the pressure to improve.

Lastly, I thank my family, particularly my parents, Ronald and Katherine Bozelko. Along with typist extraordinaire Patti Benni (who has been unofficially annexed to the Bozelko family), they have been my secretaries, making calls, shipping manuscripts. Both my parents know well the unfairness that has dogged me during my incarceration, and they have walked through this experience lockstep with me. The encouragement of my sisters and brothers-in-law, Paul and Alana Choquette and Christopher and Jana Simmons, has proved invaluable, especially hearing stories about my beautiful and brilliant nieces and nephew, Alair Choquette, Paul Choquette IV, and Mair Simmons.

Thank you everyone. I will be coming back down the river soon.

Prosecutor

She dropped her scales
      left them on the floor
      terrain of justice
and sauntered to me
      asked me to dance
      with cotton blindfold
She couldn't even see me—why extend
      the invitation?
I declined

          said no
I'm sinful so
          I'm clumsy
I can't do it so
      I stayed on the wall

Then she dropped her blindfold
      yelled to me
Why won't you dance?
      I can see you now
      I see right through
Your sins make you nimble—
      they will not hold you back for this
      task that I ask

The dance is called prosecution
criminals, your future partners—
you always pick the right one
because like recognizes like

Sometimes they trip on her
      tinny scales
But I know where they are so
      I lead them around

          And dip them at will

Public Defender

My assistance is
        In-effective
No grin, no chuckles
No wins, no brass knuckles

Just meet 'em
        plead 'em
Stamp the file closed

I'm appointed by the state
usually too late
        to help
Doesn't bother me
        that the workload's light
I still get to go home at night

Just meet 'em
        plead 'em
Stamp the file closed

My clients are not refined
Neither ladies nor gents
        They're poor
Doesn't bother me
        the poor man's plight
I don't live in urban blight

Just meet 'em
        plead 'em
Stamp the file closed

Canons dictate I must
act with zeal
But it's easier just to
make a deal
        So I do
Maybe some day
        I'll put up a fight
Am I up to the challenge? No, not quite

Just meet 'em
        plead 'em

CLOSED

Private Attorney

Reasons for the good of my pocket:

Heavy cubes of student loan debt lacking handles
Memories of bullies that appear like quadruplicate sunspots
Repeat whiners resisting rules
Bitter envies, Prada loafers, Thomas Pink shirts
Looks of seductive shock at my black Amex
Lying witnesses, abusive husbands
Grievances unfounded
        still stinging.

Reasons for the good of the public:

Inimitable smell inside a library
Heft of tomes, uneven ink explaining history
The grateful abrasion of parents who cared
Logic and rigor unmatched
Chances limited only by myself
Inequity that so outpaces policy—ever present
        forever elusive

Judge

Uprighting
    the slopes from
    behind black linen

A finger poised too firmly on scales
    leaves children alone
    and defendants prone
        all cut to the bone

Was this what they meant by
    res judicata?
Matters decided are done? Tale told?
Was this what I meant when
    I pledged to uphold?

To upright, to uphold
To fight or to fold
Cases grow cold
While clashes get old

Conflict is drama, but
        is it
           fair?

Decisions
     Decisions

    Do they know I don't care?

Witness

it's a circus
　　a whole circus
　　　　and nothing but a circus

cost of admission is
　　admission
　　　　to guilt
　　　　to truth
　　　　to bias

admit you don't know
　　who is a friend or who's a foe
admit you didn't see
　　if it was him or it was me
admit he never went
　　　　it's not straight, it's bent
　　the car had no dent
　　　　it's not stolen, it's lent
that letter was never sent
　　But that's not what I meant!

testimony is performance
　　words fly through the air
　　accountability does acrobatics
recollections, long mounts of
absent-minded elephants

lawyers with large shoes
　　wear greasepaint
　　toss buckets of verbal confetti
　　seducing the mind yearning for fools

ethics are tiny tricycles
ridden in circles, seeking response
then they become magicians
　　making facts appear where
　　　　once were none

I, their lovely assistant
　　enter on a liberty horse
　　hand them my words for justice
　　　　greatest show on earth

Judicial Marshall

Watch her, stay near her
        don't let her get away

gangs in chains
           file in and I
           take their hidden apples

I shepherd her through
        locked shafts
        secret halls
        seat her and stand

        to wait
        like
        they wait

if justice delayed is justice denied,
        then my day's name is denial

elderly men with bent backs
        teeter in and I
        can't find them their canes.

pregnant women with arched bellies
        shift in and I
        can't take their fear

she may be slow but her grain is fine

but in the meantime

don't forget
           to watch her, stay near her
        don't let her get away

Defendant

Here lies the defendant
Born at jury selection
Died at the verdict
Buried at sentencing

Beloved taxpayer and census subject
He came to trial
and leaves three young descendants
    Tad of self-esteem
    Faith in the system and
    Penny—his last one

He is predeceased by millions of others who
thought the truth would exert influence on the
fulcrum
of justice

In lieu of flowers
memorial contributions can be made
to any private correctional enterprise

He will be missed
                RIP
              Retribution
              Isolation
              Punishment

Forensic Psychiatrist

Criminal prosecution offers NO OUTLET until the
INTERSECTION of law and medicine

Riding my degrees, I cruise HIDDEN DRIVEWAYS
of abnormal behavior, holding the road through those SHARP
CURVES of psychosis

Seeing patients on the couch is PEDESTRIAN, CROSSING
the criminal mind my specialty

I pose questions
    flash inkblots
        inventory personalities
            for hours and hours
        miles of my time marked by explanations
    The Freemasons made me do it
        I just blacked out
    I was in the war
        I hadn't slept for days
    I did not kill my wife
        I never thought they'd catch me

They drone on so I
TAKE A BREAK, STAY AWAKE FOR SAFETY'S SAKE
    I might miss malingerers

Prosecutors are SLIPPERY WHEN WET behind the ears
    incapable of philosophical LANE SHIFTS
    they think I YIELD to guesses

Experienced prosecutors know you'd have to be crazy
to break the law

So I MERGE their ideas with mine, talk about
    HOSPITALS

Explain that defendants are not CHILDREN AT PLAY
in the tough games of
        guns
            drugs
        cash
            flesh
      or fire

They live on the same street
against the DEAD END of abuse

forced to TURN onto the
          avenues of WRONG WAY

SLOW AHEAD, I CAUTION
               as the cases proceed
but sometimes I fail
illness becomes character
inside courtrooms

and then

                    NO STOPPING
          CORRECTIONAL FACILITY AHEAD

Juror

Three flies sitting on a ledge.
One decides to fly away.
How many flies are on the ledge?

Two, right? Cause one flew off? STRIKE

Umm, one. The one that left. DISMISSED FOR CAUSE

Three

Yes, I know him
          He lives next door

He's the guy with the aboveground pool
          and really long clothesline

I've no problems with him
          but we're not close

Yes, someone took my wallet from my purse
          when I was unloading groceries
          I was at the other end of the cart
          and somebody just got me

I don't consider myself a victim

Sure, I think a detective can lie.

Anybody can lie.

You just have to listen.

          ACCEPTABLE

Judge

both sides lie so I
relegate judgment to chance
can't Shepardize truth

Defendant

victims die
like sand in a sieve
death pulls into the space
when time takes off
defendants die
on the gallows of the gavel
the sand collects
and clogs
and congests
the choke point
death disembarks when there is too much
such surfeit cannot sustain

there is a life without possibility
        without options and odds
        without prospects and potential
bears an ID card reading 'Lost Heart'
        chased by a number

in California, twenty-five
North Carolina says fifteen
for Connecticut, ninety-nine
to void a life of possibility

Victim

Look out
      there's hypervigilance
be careful
      it happens again

once beaten
      twice shy
            thrice wary of others' intentions

hands extended
even in help
can be frightening
Perps encroaching
violate
the inviolable

Boundaries have been split
      and security lifted
there are two places to sit
doctor's couch or the witness stand

either way, you never escape the replay

be careful
it happens again

Reporter

Fuck the Fifth
I need more
from the downtrodden in
outermost chair

I'm tethered too
to "according"
and "alleged"
sometimes "perp"

Warrants just press releases from
avenging angels in
white phylacteries

Stories never dance
their own striptease
peeling off cover
to say what really happened

Try to disrobe them but
nary one button opens

Inmate

You will want to bring your copy of *Diary of
Anne Frank* for a nightly reminder to believe in
the essential good of humankind as the barrel of
the firearm called hate presses a hole in your
back

You will especially want to take a skin with a
dial to change its thickness and salves that save
it from creeping to decrepit

You will want to pack your regrets—all of them—
rolled tightly like T-shirts in your suitcase of
self-esteem as you will wear each of them under
your uniform every day

You must take with you icing for the cake; they
always serve cake

When you go, you will leave all of the high,
high perches you climbed to see clear and far

outside the confines of fences curving inwards
and tight mesh blocking thoughts, warnings

and bring your tiny telescope
the one you can turn
inward and look inside

not for flaws or mistakes—they've been found
--but for the tiny star whose sparkle deafens
you to the sounds of the crowd chanting for
your demise

Transport Officer

Strung like a candy necklace
six-packs of screaming Sybils
all with cookie-cutter complaints
fold into refrigerated four wheelers

a sixteen hour courier to court
that is so sour, so fetid
before the tribunal
they scramble on the floor
taking whatever falls from
a prosecutor's piñata

       caramel-coated community service
       foil-wrapped freedom
       long sentence licorice loops
       rock candy rehab
       peanut-packed probation

lucky ones with stashes sweet
go home

sentenced retains are silent
bounty in their laps
satisfied

that this will be their last incursion

Property Room Officer

Six cubic feet
Cubic foot 1:   *Uniform*
Haphazard stitching pins together
cheap cotton of elastic waist Mom jeans
so long that the hems crust with mud
and disintegrate
Cubic foot 2:   *Underwear*
Bullet busted bras
Standard issue six-inch side panel
Hanes Her Way
but it's never your way
Cubic foot 3:   *Toiletries*
Viscosity-free lotions
Plastic mirrors
Brands heretofore unheard
Cubic foot 4:   *Electronics*
5-inch screen TV that
receives one channel per inch
Diminutive Conair hairdryers
become penal E-Z Bakes
Radio receives nothing
Cubic foot 5:   *Food*
Do not live on bread alone
Peanut butter, Jamaican pork
Stolen cheese inside a Fluff jar
Aside your ramen
Cubic foot 6:   *Armor*
Shuts everything out
                    Concentrating on crochet
Leafing through legal briefs
that old saw of prison writing
Six cubic feet
All you have

Correction Officer

My job is to keep them safe
But I might fail
The inmates might reject me
I'm not ready yet
I'm afraid to tell my wife
I might get hurt
I might have to change
It might cost me my pension
I would rather die than lose that way
I don't want anyone to know that I have a problem
I can't express my feelings
I'm not allowed to talk about it
I don't have the energy anymore
Who knows where I'll end up?
I could lose my freedom for this
It's too hard to balance
I wouldn't appear powerful
If I tell, I might lose my friends
It might hurt my image
I'm not good enough—that's why I'm here

I don't trust anyone

SHIFT CHANGE

Correction Counselor

connect to outside
bridge over troubled women
get walked on daily

Prison Chaplain

        canvas tote carries
free truth for distribution
"your Father loves you"

        and he likes you, too
each hair on your head matters
        never alone, always

Visitor

Can love seep through glass
shatterproof with greasy prints?
distance magnified

Prison Doctor

In this place which was a farm
I must maintain to do no harm.

It's not easy—my hands are tied
Formularies and balance sheets my only guide

Women come in sick and then leave sicker
Unmanaged damage from drugs and liquor

Care should be the same as outside
But when I ordered tests, the nurse just sighed

"In here it's not the same
Health's not a calling but a game

Unless it's a germ that makes them die
You can do nothing—don't even try

You can order tests, creams and pills
But the state never pays those bills"

I said "They don't come to jail to be punished
Only to live here just as the judge wished"

Their punishment is coming here
But it's the death penalty for some, I fear

Can't do what I'm trained to do
First inmates die, then they sue

Scabies, MRSA, Hepatitis C
These things spread, can't they see?

To curb costs, prevention is key
But we wait for decline, how can that be?"

With fever, chills, she's sent back to her cell
The good prison doctor has a soul to sell

This bureaucracy is strong—it twists my arm
How can I maintain to do no harm?

Food Preparation Unit

Eat lunch at 10 am
Dinner is at four

Cases of celery, carrots
Hundreds of cabbages
Under knives while
Cross-cut blades mince nutrition for
Kettles boiling

Spices, then pellets, then toss into a
Chiller, wait
One hour before you
Take out
Those bags

Just in case the freezer goes down
Each meal should be staged
Recipes lay on pallets
Ready to load until someone
Yells "All in!"

Drivers disperse in refrigerated trucks
Assigned drop-offs at other prisons
Veggie patties, bologna steaks, sometimes
Even fried chicken

Food preparation unit
Runs the whole operation, it
All happens here
No one else supplies prison
Kitchens throughout the state.

Prison Mailroom

Hold vigil
for colors
or photos with signs
porn
occasional threat against state officials

Subliterate population
generates
screed
in piles of postage paid envelopes

As always
in criminal justice
anything marked by privilege
slides right through
never molested

Correction Officer

Oh Lordy!
It's Sunday
"Secure all your doors!"
My partner?
    he's crazy
He calls the girls whores.

Oh Lordy!
It's Monday
"Let me see your ID!"
Got off with
    a warning
Otherwise it'd be me.

Oh Lordy!
It's Tuesday
"Those pants are too tight!"
Sometimes
    not to slap them
Takes all of my might.

Oh Lordy!
It's Wednesday
"Do you have a pass!"
No, you're
    not a "boy"
You're a pain in my ass.

Oh Lordy!
It's Thursday
"Now bend, squat and cough!"
While I look
at my watch
to see when I get off.

Oh Lordy!
It's Friday
"Tuck in that white shirt!"
They keep on
    returning
because they can't stop the hurt.

Directives

Oh Lordy!
It's Saturday
"There's nothing else I can do."
Directives
    prevent me
but I'd like to help you

The work-week
is
    over
"Who wants overtime?"
Forget it -
    I'm leaving
for my house in East Lyme

The work-week
is
    over
Took this job 'cause it pays
Don't worry -
    You'll see me
Be back in three days

Prison Maintenance

The dishwasher's broken
The gasket is blown
The valve's leaking
Its cause unknown

D tier's dryers aren't working
And they still need dry clothes
And their washer's shaking loudly
So bring a new hose

On the sink in HIO
The cold button sticks
And Zero South's panel
Does nothing when you click

A radiator in Thompson Hall
Hisses nonstop
Food prep's printer just busted
When the ink cartridge popped

A toilet in seg
Is seeping into the ground
And look
The grits turned brown

The oven's misbehaving
It torched the hot dogs
Same thing with the kitchen pipes
It looks like they're clogged

I don't have a work order
So put in another slip
Separate form for each problem
I'll make a second trip

Don't know what you expect of me
Can't be two places at once
I'll fix whatever you want
Just call me after lunch

Prison Librarian

Dewey Decimal discharged
leaving literary looseness
Ebonics hawked as city sophistication
newspapers scanned only for astral prediction
compromised collections of classics

Prisons admit uncorrected proofs

pages inside redeemed as love coupons

trading contingent affection

happy endings sliced out

crumpled by apathy just like them

Bookplates
detail genealogy
This book belonged to
obsolescence until
charity commandeered a UPS truck
dyads scanned bar codes
left them in a prison's lobby

Social Worker

But what is social work?   You're nothing more than
                                      an operator
      he asked   the receptionist to the poor
I'll need to know if
      I am to pay the tuition   I try to help
                                    people
Social work   and help myself
      I explained   understand what I'm
is working with people
                              supposed to do
Hah! he laughed
Even the man who works
alone works with people
      someone writes his check
            checks his work
                  works through his bill
Everyone works with people

Social work
      I explained
traces the totality of human relationships
it fuses burst boundaries
      connects people with services
           services men with help
                helps women in need

No crime is a closed universe
It's just the epicenter of problems
I try to stop the ripples
      the energy from transmitting
           and only destroying more
That is what social work is
      I explained.

It sounds like you're the call center everyone rings
      When the ends don't meet
           They meet bad influences or
                Influence the innocent

Prison Nurse

public health frontline
one interface with inmates
my hands are cuffed too

Warden's Secretary

Warden's office, how may I help you?

Ma'am, your daughter's in seg, restricted housing
Apparently, she snatched an officer's wig
off her head and
set it ablaze with a contraband lighter
Did she get a ticket?
Yes, that does mean a ticket
 I'll give the warden your message

Warden's office, how may I help you?

Sir, your daughter's in mental health
Q15 status
because she tried to hurt herself
No, as in attempt suicide
No, I don't know how
I'll give the warden your message

Warden's office?

No, she never got the package
We found heroin
taped inside a Jersey Shore calendar
sent in from an inmate's girlfriend
So we cannot let anything else in

How may I help you?

No, sir, you are not an approved visitor
Why? Because of the protective order instituted from the
last time you beat her
And the fact that she sits here because she robbed the bank
with you
I'll give the warden your message

No, sir. we do not replace stolen do-rags
Yes, your daughter can have a free pap smear
Well, Mr. Bozelko, if you just mailed it yesterday
Absconder means leaving parole
Let me give the warden this message

Warden

Crime is a growth stock
syndicates open every day
open orders invite the oppressed into confinement
orders never cancelled

police raids round up
numbers for a
judicial bull market

accidental trader
in his satellite office
away from the prisoners trafficked on the
       trading floor of the courtroom

after the initial public offering—the arraignment
penny stocks remain in the stockade
police blotters the big board
indexes list not points but years, months, lost life

banker stuffs the single slip
of numbers 33-04-45
into his silk shirt's pocket
the combination to the human safe

Deputy Warden

empowered to act
in warden's stead for safety
of secrets staff hide

Correction Captain

Only me steering
one inch on the wheel
points miles off course

Wardens and deps
don't ride the swells
rather they meet
      greet
      lead
      cheat

At the helm, abandoned
like the Gorton's fisherman
trust from above and below
slides to puddles off my slicker
pools at my feet

because I cannot use it all
administer, operate and program

we can't use it all

Disciplinary Investigator

your behavior
is scrawny scribble
snaking between
two concepts, divides them:
the correctional institution and
the penitentiary

in the correctional institution
serve yourself by serving others
fuse your will to the rules
and learn to derive
satisfaction from it

the penitentiary
imprisons you in your habits
allows treacherous public enemies to ripen

stains you with
margarine
pilfered in your panties

never deign to work for 75 cents
instead disobey

reinforcing your addiction buying pills shed
of their enteric coating
by another inmate's mouth

projecting anger
disregard of reprobates
foul-mouthed furies
like the fact that you sit across from my desk
                              is my fault

Records Captain

end of sentence date
breaks the chain to boomerang
back at our front door

Clerk

Very few perks
to being the clerk
part of my work
is placating jerks
each judge's quirks
drive me berserk
and the lawyers? They lurk
around my desk and smirk
trying to irk

condescension reminding:
"You're just the clerk."

Correction Officer

I used to be nice
used to think twice

thought myself a monarch
until anger, spirit diminishing
rippled under a clenched jaw
snapping reflexes

needy neophytes
        manipulative motherfuckers
arrogant from unabated abuse
think they seduce me
flashes of whiteness
dimpled chicken skin

to make a sale
where I'm the refund

it's all done to get me back

Department of Correction Press Liaison

Department policy is up, up and away
    Screw up
        Cover up
           Then run away

It is department policy
to keep all inmates safe
        except when they die

It is department policy
to terminate employees
who engage in sexual misconduct
        when the cameras catch them

It is department policy
to provide an environment
for inmates that fosters
rehabilitation and successful re-entry to our society
        when they haven't escaped up the street
        to do a dine and dash
        at the Lyme Tavern

I cannot comment on pending litigation
so I wish all inmates would sue
then "no comment" would issue

no facts to take form
against microphones
sift from my life those
harmful words of responsibility

bidding officials to protect themselves
from onlookers gazing past the obvious
to the pattern within.

Governor

My signature's a sickle
of sodium thiopental

Sanguine bloodlust funds this
system

Whoever said revenge is best
served cold knew
the chilled, steel gurney under
the man sentenced to die
arm outstretched for calibration of
                                        killing

Buck stops with me
makes me rich with regret.

Parole Board Member

your past predicts best
what you will do when you leave
so I guess you're screwed

Inmate

The Inmate Request System provides an informal
way of obtaining information or a written answer to a
question or an issue about a policy, procedure or
practice from a staff member.

Request sounds so formal
                    It's really a plea
                            a query
                        a tirade
                    a say-can't-you-see
        It's really complaint
                accusation
            allegation
        negation
                Or really direction
                        rejection
                            infectious hearsay
                                With something to say
                        Three words rumble past
            "Well, then write!"

        So I did.

.

About the Author

CHANDRA BOZELKO is a Princeton graduate and currently incarcerated at York Correctional Institution in Niantic, Connecticut. Her essays have appeared in *Commonweal* and the *New Haven Independent.*

About the Editors

SUSAN NAGELSEN is the Director of the Writing Program at New England College. She is widely published as an essayist, fiction, and creative nonfiction writer. Most recently, her work has appeared in *The New Plains Review* and *Epiphanymagazine.com.* She is the author/editor of *Exiled Voices, Portals of Discovery.* Her writing has also appeared in *The Henniker Review, The Poets' Touchstone*, and a number of newspapers and academic journals. Writers who are incarcerated have captured her interest for the past twenty-five years. She serves as an associate editor of *The Journal of Prisoners on Prison* and a senior consulting editor for BleakHouse Publishing.

CHARLES HUCKELBURY is a poet and essayist. His two books, *Distant Thunder* and *Tales from the Purple Penguin*, were both published by BleakHouse Publishing, where he is a senior consulting editor. He is the recipient of four PEN America prizes for nonfiction and fiction, and is the reviewer/editor of *Huck's Picks*, the newsletter for Prisons Foundation in Washington, DC.

About the Designers

LIZ CALKA is an award-winning designer and photographer with a degree in Visual Media and Graphic Design from American University. As Art Director at BleakHouse Publishing, she has designed covers and layouts for a number of BleakHouse publications including books and magazines. She also created and maintains the BleakHouse website.

SONIA TABRIZ graduated from American University (2010) *summa cum laude* with University Honors, with a B.A. in Law and Society and a B.A. in Psychology. She received the Outstanding Scholarship at the Undergraduate Level award for her award-winning works of fiction, legal commentaries, artwork, presentations, university-wide accolades, and academic achievement. Tabriz graduated with a J.D. from The George Washington University Law School, where she served as a Writing Fellow and Editor-in-Chief of the *Public Contract Law Journal.* Tabriz is the Managing Editor of BleakHouse Publishing and designs the text for various publications.

RACHEL TERNES is an honors undergraduate student at American University majoring in psychology and minoring in French and studio arts. Her passion for creating art is rivaled only by her interest in using her artistic skill to promote causes of social justice. As Chief Creative Officer for BleakHouse Publishing, Ternes designs visuals for press releases and publicity, and contributes to the visual design and illustration of publications.

CPSIA information can be obtained at www.ICGtesting.com
Printed in the USA
BVOW05s1645100314

346973BV00006B/38/P